LOVE, LIFE, GOD AND EVERYTHING IN BETWEEN

A Collection of Poems

Maggie A. Walker

Table of contents

Chapter 1: LOVE

TREASURE

Just like my star

Just like my star

Sparkling in this tender night

I love to hear

the way you say, "My Dear"

You are everything

this world brings

that's why you are

My Prince Charming

loving you everyday

with the vital love you give

wondering why I love you

just the way I do

Holding me close

looking into my eyes

makes me melt and want you,

sometimes I wonder why

Where you have been
All these years
Your eyes say
"With you I'm here to stay"
So that's why I love you
All the very same

WINDS

It is like volcanic eruption

with hot burning lava

It's like fire

as orange as embers

It's like a cloak

lacey yet so tough

It's like the moon

shining a little too soon

It's like the forest

united with greenly goddess

It is like knife

sharp when given a dive

It's like man

wise with lingering mind

It's like the ocean

wavy but so real

It's like hunger

with frantic desire

It's like sand

a deadly mate

It's like rain

leaving a daisy trail

Its like owl in the morning

blind and so dull

It's like music

soft and romantic

It's like nature

with very simple pleasure

most of all, it's like you

that makes my heart beats

LIFE LINE

Life so strange and weird
giving me a heart
I so much dared
full of strange emotion
and enthusiasm
So, I thought it seems
falling in and out of love
Is so strange
and makes me amaze
there's nothing I wish for
but a true touch
…touch that melts a heart
giving it a meaningful beat
that's will always
make it succeed
there's something I long for
…is a heart I call my very own
take everything it has sown
just like a farmer
who nurses its crop

praying, watering, weeding it up
Is the love I so long for

CONNECTION

I'm in love

swimming in it

In love with who

that's the question that woos

love so sweet and feeble

love so strong yet subtle

clothing your sweetness

adorned in your richness

move to the rhythm

the beat of the tune

In you, there's no harm

though your being

Is known to hurt

so sweet yet bitter,

Is your thought

dancing so sparkly

Is your molecules

touching me

In the tete – tete tune

beginning from the end

ending from the end

you make the morning radiates

and the night dazzling sparkle

like the Egyptian night

So romantically strong is your thought

swimming passionately

In my heart

crying out, reaching out,

calling out

to the only one, it belongs

EROTIC

A day when I walked

I walked in the day

a season of love arose

this was a

lovely spring of roses

also an autumn full of doves

a long harsh icy winter lingered

around the lazy

but beautiful summer

all these seasons

bring joy so sweet

all these seasons

make me alive, you see

all these seasons

are so real and true

but none of these

are as daisy as you

hope your wondrous ways

won't fade away

DREAM BUT TRUE

Your love is more like a dream

So real to me than

the rainbow's blue

your grace is an amazing touch

So smoothen than

the richest balm

you're my life and breath

living in me so real

You are my beauty and spring

My Prince Charming

and that's why I sing

My lovely pearl

My only jewel

Holding unto you, can't let go

cause you are my everything

when all my hopes are gone

when all my dreams fade

Your ray of love

shines and radiates

into my heart

Why ……... but why
do you love me?
I give you so little of mine
but you never mind
sometimes I think
you are a fool
I threw your love away
into a dirty filthy trash bin
and go out searching
for "true" love
yet you dust it and hand it
to me with more truthful words
how could I have left unseen
the true and real love
which you gave to me
but now I know
you're so true
So true…is your love

COLOR OF LOVE

Deeper than the blue sea

Is my love for you, you see

higher than any mountain

Is the beat of my heart to sustain

the raging sea and dark night

cannot move the frantic love

Ride with me

on the magic carpet

cause it'll take us

to our land of love

not of conditions and serpents

listen to the movement

to the rhythm of my body

perfect twist to the touch

of your love

Drink from the slimy ocean

of my freshness

and it will fill you

and you'll think

touch the redness of my soul

and let your yellowness
twine with mine
let's live in the forever
greenness of our love

COLORS

Your hands touch me
leaving a rose feeling and needs
your lips touch me
leaving a bluebell
mind that leads
your body touches me
leaving rainbow behind so thick
when you kiss me
It leaves a pinkish song to sing
you are a perfect love
can't leave, 'cos ever sealed
just wanting to say
love me in my very way

AMOUR

From the moment I saw you
my whole world changed,
the stars stone brighter
the falling rain
had new meaning
the moment I saw you
my heart and soul, you won
you own the very quality,
My love and gem
you're my desire, my love
and my best friend
each day, each night
I am lost in thoughts of you
you, my prince
are my very being
the moment I saw you,
I knew my heart will follow
cos you leave me breathless
my virtue, sparkle, beauty
naivete is all you

Listen to what my heart has to say
cos what my words
cannot express
Is said, through my peace
my hopes and dreams
I share with you
you are the one I give
my body and soul
the only one I seek to know
my desire, the one I worship
with my heart
my, lover and one,
my sun and my moon

Chapter 2: LIFE

FILLING AND FEELING

What is life

that we have to live it

What is food

that we have to eat it

What is friend

that we have to have it

What is education

that we have to study it

What is beauty

that we have to flaunt it

What is wealth

that we have to acquire it

What is knowledge

that we have to want to

What is love

that we have to share it

What us power

that we have to get it

What is in this world

that you won't later loose

vanity upon vanity

a writer once wrote

certainly the world

Is vanity upon vanity

REAL ME

There was a time I knew

exactly what I wanted

There was a time I could

specify that little need in me

There was a time

everything had its place

There was a time the line

I could clearly trace

There was a time

I was happy and gay

There was a time even

a glace was more than a tale

There was a time there was

something to save

There was a time I was

actually my very me

though it may seem so frenzy

here and now is just loving me

SONG OF FREEDOM

I developed in a slave world
I was raised a slave
clothed a slave
ate a slave
breath like a slave
drank like a slave
sang with slaves
treated like a slave
dance like a slave
but not born a slave
thinking of all these
makes me fragile and stained
but I know one thing for sure
I will never ever die a slave

TASTE AND THE FEEL

It's full of mysteries

hatred and darkness

Its life but

life itself is a problem

Its something

you love and hate

you like and dislike

you own and lose

Its life and death

It is like drama

you have to play your part

and play it well

It's full of beauty that

you don't know how to use it

It's full of happenings

that makes you laugh and cry

turn you to someone or no one

put you somewhere or nowhere

it's full of different behaviors

which sometimes frustrate you

and sometimes gives you happiness

but most of all it doesn't care

HOPE

Hope, Hope, Hope
What can we say
a world of darkness
troubles and temptations
horrible and miserable things
a world of rich and poor
be confident
trust yourself
you can make it
don't lose Hope
just pray and let him take control
remember
you can do it without "them"
If you know what I mean

MESSY

My feeling is afloat

so my stomach is a bloat

emotionally not strong

but mentally not wrong

I have slipped and

the joints shifted

though healing and

cleaning get nearer

healing is slow

and the scar very clear

my world has stopped – tis

so is my only heart

It simply stopped

ticking and wishing

nothing seems to make it work

so why try to repair

what's done

It's easier to stay bloat

when everything hard is afloat

living is wishful thinking

so why dance when sinking
when the sun is not bright
and the moon has lost its light
why try when
nothing is to lose
and letting go – no heart
and definitely no song
but I'm holding on to the one
to the one I know is exact

Chapter 3: GOD

YOU

You're my joy
and my song
You're my peace
to my heart beat
You're my salt
to everything
even my thoughts
You're life
to myself at last
You are strong
which sparkle in my dark
You're there
when I need a friend
You are my everything that keeps me within
You're the light
that brightens my life
You're the song

I love to sing all day long

You're near

when I need you to be there

You're the west

In the morning when I am set

You are my strength and grace

when i'm sad in the race

You're my faith

to push me through

night and day

You are always the same

and to this, I would say

there's no friend and love

as perfect as you

MY WAY – HIS WAY

I talk of you in hate

but you speak to me in love

I pray to you in anger

but you answer me with gladness

I gave you an attitude

that doesn't care

but you gave me

a caring ear

I speak of hate and dislike

You speak of love and like you

what else do I want from you

for you are God

and the living on alone

EIGHT "WILLS" OF GOD

I will forgive you

I will love you

I will live with you

I will stay with you

I will help you

I will guide you

I will stand by you

I will life you up

and these are my will

to them who love

and respect me

obey my commandment

THE BIG BOOK

You are the unseen word
the fragile truth
You are the light
that reveals every man's dream
You are the mind
that travels thousands and
thousands of mile
the very true reality
that looks like the early dew
very imagination tries to incline
but none can
comprehend the line
You are the very
and everything
In you every living has its being

Chapter 4: EVERYTHING IN BETWEEN

PARENT

You are my life

because you gave me life

because you love me indeed

you do your best

In order to give me rest

you feel my hurt

when im dull and hurt

you will do anything for me

In order to be safe and secure

your bosom is filled with love

given to me just

like a perfect parent does

you are my everything

through thick and thin

you are perfect gift from God

who is only the true source

and when I scream and fuss

you never lose your temper

when you ought to you never

your strength is like

that of a thousand men

but gentle and soft even then

your faith I try to comprehend

which I know will help

you to the end

thank you for the love

and affection you gave

will never forget

even unto my grave

FRIENDS

Dearest friend
this is just to write to you
what is in my heart
which is very true
what i'm really going
to miss you
but I know that
the days will stay blue
I thank God for Jesus Christ
who has done everything
In His very might
who has made me know you
a friend that is so good
though I met you so late
that's God own perfect date

SOME STUPID SAYING

"What goes up and

never comes down"

oh no, some rich do

go poor some day

the sky's the limit they say

but nobody ever

got there till this day

a word is enough for the wise

but a word is never there

before an experience

nemesis will catch up with the evil

that's done when the hurt is deep and full

a friend in need is a friend indeed

never believe that

or it will make you bleed

rome was not built in a day

yea right, when you have

the money you can in a day

make hay while the sun shines

so that the tyrants can

have them alright

a good name is better

than silver and Gold

but if you have them

everyone listens to tales told.

A SHIP CALLED FRIEND

Life is not a bed of roses
we all have our ups and downs
we all want someone who holds
to hold us up when we drown
that's why they say
a friend in need
Is a friend indeed
a friend to take our pains away
a friend who never fails
God is everything that stays
but hope our friendship
will work
a little magic, all the same